Marvin Steps Out

Tom Armstrong

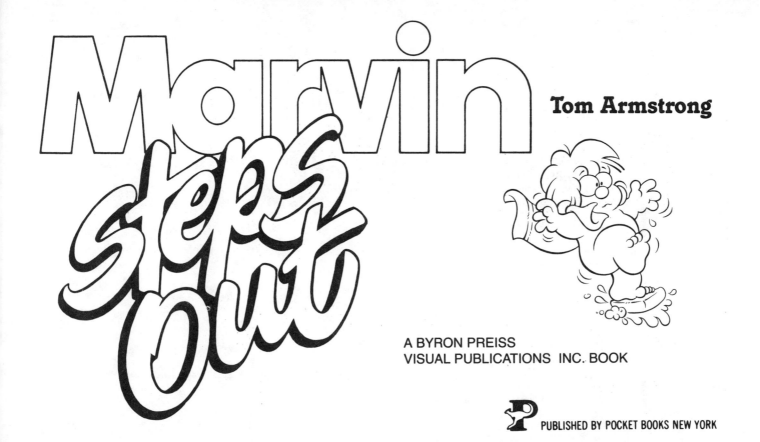

A BYRON PREISS
VISUAL PUBLICATIONS INC. BOOK

P PUBLISHED BY POCKET BOOKS NEW YORK

An *Original* publication of POCKET BOOKS

*The comic strips in this book have been previously published
in syndication.*

POCKET BOOKS, a division of Simon & Schuster, Inc.,
1230 Avenue of the Americas, New York, N.Y. 10020

ISBN: 0-671-60703-0

First Pocket Books trade paperback printing November, 1985

10 9 8 7 6 5 4 3 2 1

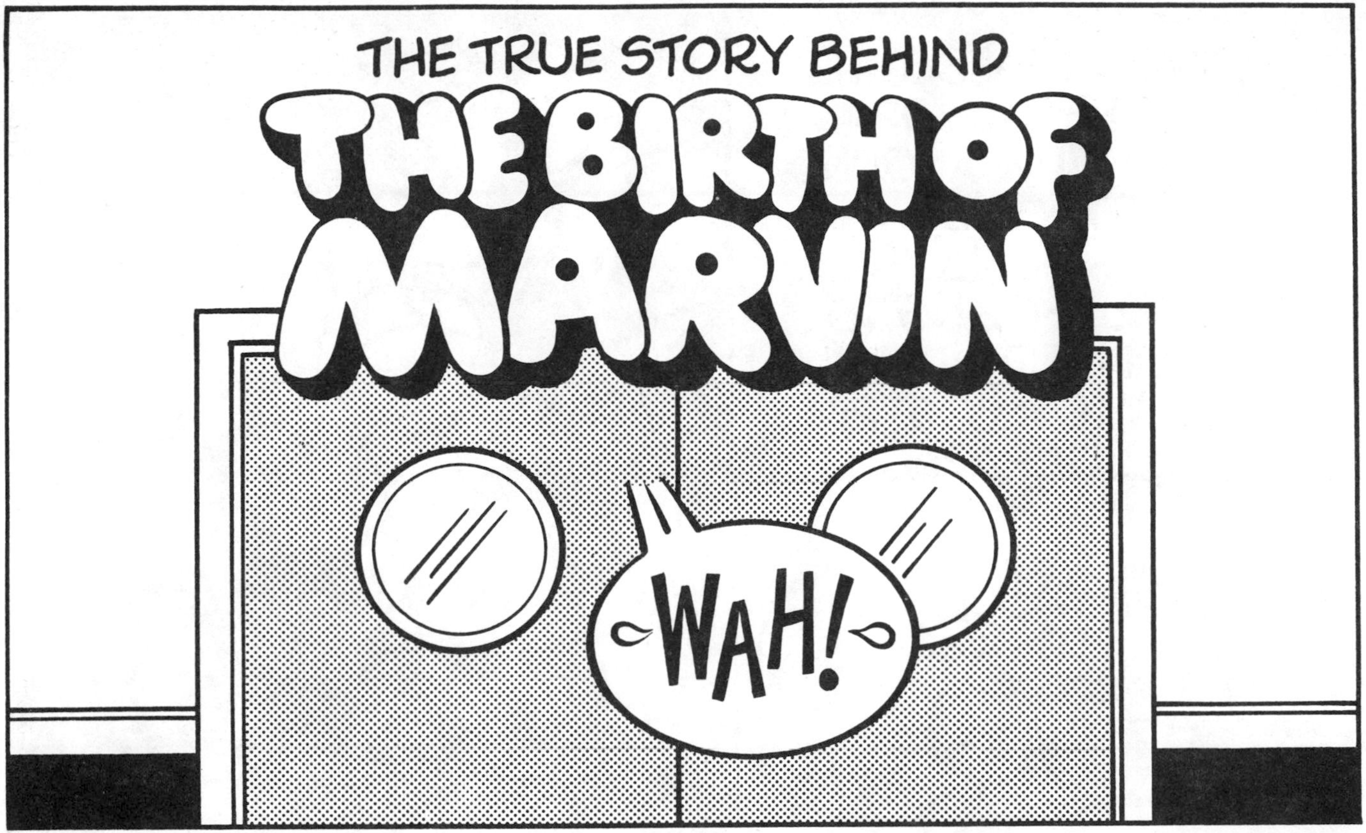
THE TRUE STORY BEHIND
THE BIRTH OF MARVIN
WAH!

OUR STORY BEGINS IN THE FALL OF 1981 WITH A YOUNG CARTOONIST FRANTICALLY STRUGGLING TO COME UP WITH A NEW COMIC STRIP CHARACTER.

THIS COULD TAKE AWHILE

AND JUST AS SUDDENLY, HE WAS STRUCK WITH A NICE, JUICY LAWSUIT FOR COPYRIGHT INFRINGEMENT.

I TRIED TO WARN HIM

ALRIGHT, SO MAYBE IT WASN'T SUCH A GREAT IDEA

GLUE

NEXT, HE CAME UP WITH A COMIC STRIP ABOUT A BUNCH OF PEOPLE WORKING IN A GROCERY STORE...

IT'LL NEVER SELL

JUST IN THE NICK OF TIME HE WAS SAVED BY A STUPENDOUS INSPIRATION...

AND A STOMACH PUMP

EUREKA!! I'VE GOT THE PERFECT IDEA!

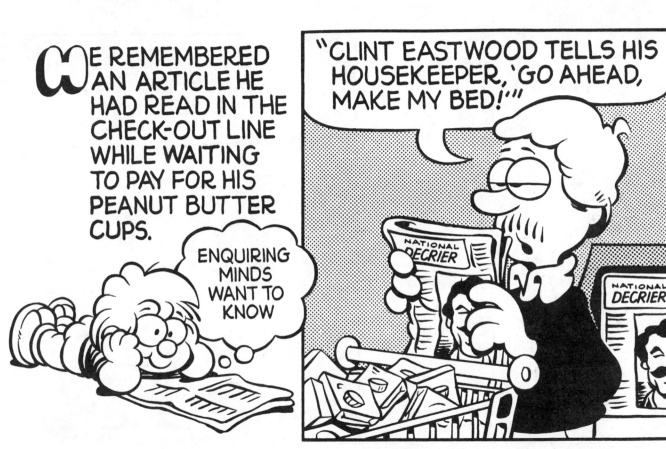

HOW'D YOU LIKE A FAT AND SASSY KNUCKLE SANDWICH?

FEED ME

THEN HE ADDED SOME SUPPORTING CHARACTERS TO THE CAST...

I JUST KEEP THEM AROUND FOR A FEW LAUGHS

MARVIN'S PARENTS

HIS GRANDPARENTS

JEFF & JENNY MILLER

BITSY THE DOG

...AND HIS COUSIN MEAGAN

YEOW! OUCH!

OOCH! OUCH!

TOM ARMSTRONG

ONE SHOULD NEVER WEAR SHORTS AROUND A BABY THAT'S LEARNING TO PULL UP

I CAN'T LEAVE YOU ALONE FOR FIVE MINUTES, MARVIN

YOU'VE GOT STAMPS STUCK ALL OVER YOU. MAYBE I SHOULD MAIL YOU TO SOMEONE ELSE

TOM ARMSTRONG

OF COURSE, I'D HAVE TO SEND YOU BULK RATE

CUTE, REAL CUTE

SPALOOP!

YOU'RE SUCH A SWEET BABY

NOTHING'S TOO GOOD FOR SUCH A FINE GRANDSON

I LOVE A WOMAN WHO UNDERSTANDS ME

BEA AND I ARE REALLY ENJOYING BEING GRANDPARENTS

MARVIN IS OUR WHOLE WORLD

GEE, I NEVER WOULD HAVE GUESSED

TOM ARMSTRONG

YOU KNOW IT'S GOING TO BE A COLD WINTER...

WHEN IT'S ONLY SEPTEMBER...

AND YOU FIND A PENGUIN ESTABLISHING RESIDENCY IN YOUR WADING POOL

Tom Armstrong

EVERYTHING ALWAYS SMELLS SO CLEAN AND FRESH RIGHT AFTER A RAIN

SLURP! SLURP!

TALK ABOUT YOUR EXTRA-ABSORBENT DIAPER...

Tom Armstrong

SPLASH!
SPLASH!

NOW THAT'S WHAT I CALL A QUICK COLD SNAP

TOM ARMSTRONG

I'VE NOTICED THAT YOU NEVER SEE FLIES WHEN IT GETS COLD

I GUESS THEY FLY SOUTH FOR THE WINTER

TOM ARMSTRONG

VAMPIRES ALWAYS SURROUND THEMSELVES WITH OBEDIENT SLAVES

COUNT MARVIN IS NO EXCEPTION

MEET MY ZOMBIES

TOM ARMSTRONG

IT'S COMMON KNOWLEDGE THAT GARLIC WILL WARD OFF VAMPIRES

HOWEVER, IT'S BEEN COUNT MARVIN'S EXPERIENCE...

THAT BROCCOLI CAN BE EQUALLY EFFECTIVE

TOM ARMSTRONG

THE SECRET TO A SUCCESSFUL HALLOWEEN....

TRICK OR TREAT

IS GOING TO HOUSES WHERE THEY KNOW YOU

I GIVE UP

EVERY ONE OF YOUR SHIRTS HAS FOOD STAINS ON THE FRONT

I PREFER TO THINK OF IT AS PERSONALIZED MONOGRAMMING

EVERYBODY ALWAYS TALKS ABOUT "FOOTBALL WIDOWS"...

TOM ARMSTRONG

BUT NOBODY EVER MENTIONS US "ORPHANS"

...JACK FELL DOWN AND BROKE HIS CROWN

AND JILL CAME TUMBLING AFTER

SOUNDS LIKE GROUNDS FOR A NICE JUICY LAWSUIT TO ME.

TOM ARMSTRONG

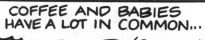

I KNOW MOM MEANS WELL

SHE JUST WANTS TO KEEP AN EYE ON ME SO I DON'T GET HURT

TOM ARMSTRONG

BUT I THINK INSTALLING SECURITY MIRRORS IN THE FAMILY ROOM IS GOING TOO FAR

MUNCH! MUNCH!

TOM ARMSTRONG

SPLAT!

I THINK I LIKED IT BETTER WHEN MARVIN ONLY DRANK FROM A BOTTLE

I'VE NOTICED...

THAT IN MARVIN'S HANDS...

TOM ARMSTRONG

THERE'S NO SUCH THING AS A "SLOW KETCHUP"

I DECIDED TO ADD A DECORATOR TOUCH TO MY CRIB...

PULL!

TOM ARMSTRONG

MINI-BLINDS

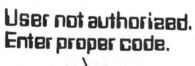

NOW THAT I'VE LOGGED INTO MOM AND DAD'S CHRISTMAS SHOPPING LIST, I'LL TAKE A LOOK AT WHAT THEY'VE BUDGETED TO SPEND ON ME

TAP TAP

Toys: $15
Clothes: $35

THAT DOESN'T SEEM FAIR

Toys: $48
Clothes: $2

MUCH BETTER

TAP TAP TAP

IT SEEMS KIND OF TACKY OF MY PARENTS TO ASSIGN A DOLLAR VALUE TO MY CHRISTMAS HAPPINESS

I'LL JUST RE-PROGRAM A MORE FLEXIBLE BUDGET

TAP TAP TAP

1983 Christmas Budget.
Subject: Marvin.
Nothing is too good for such a sweet little boy.

'TIS THE SEASON TO BE ADORABLE

Tom Armstrong

YOU GET MORE GIFTS THAT WAY

WELL, MARVIN...

Tom Armstrong

I SEE YOU'VE BEEN WATCHING FOR SANTA'S ARRIVAL

HOW'D SHE KNOW?

COME HERE, MARVIN, I WANT TO COMB YOUR HAIR

SWOOOSH

I THINK THAT'S WHAT'S KNOWN AS RUNNING A COMB THROUGH YOUR HAIR

TOM ARMSTRONG

I DECIDED TO GO FORMAL FOR DINNER TONIGHT

BLACK TIE...

AND BLACK DIAPER

TOM ARMSTRONG

HMMM...

THIS MUST BE ONE OF THOSE "ONE SIZE FITS ALL" HATS

Tom Armstrong

WHEN IT'S COLD OUTSIDE...

GROWN-UPS OFTEN WEAR STOCKING CAPS

BABIES WEAR BODY STOCKINGS

Tom Armstrong

WHAT'S THE MATTER WITH MARVIN?

HE SPENT THE DAY AT HIS GRANDPARENTS...

AND NOW HE'S GOING THROUGH SUGAR WITHDRAWAL

TOM ARMSTRONG

I DON'T KNOW WHY MOM GETS SO UPSET WHEN I SUCK MY THUMB

SLURP! SLURP!

IF IT WASN'T GOOD FOR YOU...

GOD WOULD HAVE PUT A WARNING LABEL ON IT

TOM ARMSTRONG

UH, OH...

I'VE GOTTA GET A ROLLBAR FOR THIS ROCKER

DAD'S REALLY PROUD

HE ENTERED SOMETHING I DID IN THE LOCAL ART SHOW

MY BIB TOOK FIRST PLACE

KISSY!
KISSY!

I'M PRACTICING MY KISSING

WHEN I GROW UP I WANT TO BE A QUIZ SHOW HOST

WAAAAAA!

DON'T TELL ME YOUR DIAPER NEEDS CHANGING AGAIN!

WAAAAAAA!

IT'S A DIRTY JOB, BUT SOMEONE HAS TO DO IT

TOM ARMSTRONG

HERE'S MARVIN'S PRESCRIPTION FOR HIS COUGH, MR. MILLER

THAT'LL BE TWENTY-FIVE DOLLARS, PLEASE

NOW I KNOW WHAT THEY MEAN BY "COUGHING UP THE MONEY"

TOM ARMSTRONG

WHEN YOU'RE A BABY, YOU GET TO HUG YOUR TEDDY BEAR

WHEN YOU GROW UP...

TOM ARMSTRONG

YOU HAVE TO SETTLE FOR A WIFE

I DON'T LIKE TO WEAR SOCKS

I PREFER MY SHOES UNLINED

TOM ARMSTRONG

I'VE JUST COME UP WITH THE PERFECT INVENTION FOR BABIES, MARVIN

HERE, TRY IT ON

TOM ARMSTRONG

A DIAPER MADE OUT OF SPONGE!

TOO BAD YOUR BRAIN IS MADE OUT OF SPONGE

CAUTION
THIS SLIDE
MAY BE
SLIPPERY
DURING
ICY
CONDITIONS

TOM ARMSTRONG

I'M WEARING MY NEW WINTER DIAPERS

THEY'RE QUILTED WITH DUCK DOWN

TOM ARMSTRONG

THE MOON ISN'T AS BRIGHT AS THE SUN

I GUESS THAT'S BECAUSE IT'S A NIGHT-LIGHT

TOM ARMSTRONG

⊚☆ʘⱣ#⚹!⚡‼

OUR TV SURE SAYS A LOT OF NAUGHTY WORDS

I GUESS THAT'S WHY MOM AND DAD MAKE IT STAND IN THE CORNER

TOM ARMSTRONG

Next!

(Coming Spring, 1986, from Pocket Books)

Cartoonist Tom Armstrong is by no means a newcomer to the art field. At the ripe old age of five he drew a comic strip about camels, and from those humble beginnings sprang the comic genius behind Tom's later—and more human—syndicated cartoon creations, MARVIN and JOHN DARLING.

"I started cartooning probably before I could talk," Tom says. "My dad was an aspiring cartoonist, and after watching him for a while, I started drawing, too."

After four years of high school art training, Tom entered the University of Evansville, serving as the staff cartoonist for the campus paper, The Crescent, with a weekly strip about campus life called "Two-S." He graduated with a bachelor's degree in fine arts and several art awards under his belt: the Helen Morris Outstanding Senior Award in oil painting, the University of Evansville alumni Certificate of Excellence, the Medal of Merit for "significant contributions to collegiate journalism," second place for Best Editorial Cartoons from the Pi Delta Epsilon national journalism fraternity and the Indiana Collegiate Press Association's Best Editorial Cartoon award.

From there, Tom got into free-lance illustrating: He's drawn for many well-known publications, including **The Saturday Evening Post** and **The National Review.**

Tom has also done a good deal of work with advertising agencies, developing animated cartoons, multi-media slide presentations, animated TV spots and print ads for national companies from RCA to Sears and many more. He is a three-time recipient of the Golden Circle Award for "achieving the highest standards of advertising and selling excellence in worldwide competition."

Tom's first venture into comic strip syndication came in 1979 with JOHN DARLING, done in tandem with FUNKY WINKERBEAN creator Tom Batiuk. DARLING stars a fictional TV talk show host, his co-workers and celebrity guests (real-life celebrities drawn in caricature by Armstrong).

MARVIN, featuring the precocious red-haired star of Marvin Steps Out, followed in August, 1982. The character's popularity on the comics pages soon led to equal success in licensing and merchandising.

A prime-time television special, produced by Southern Star Studios, is in production for CBS.

Tom, his wife, Glenda, and two children, Jonathan and Jennifer (who also serve as a gold mine of ideas for MARVIN's antics) make their home in southern Indiana.